A Kind of Flourishing

poems by

Angela Griner

Finishing Line Press
Georgetown, Kentucky

A Kind of Flourishing

For my mother and father, my best friend and partner Kyle in this redemptive season, my extended family, and all the backyard creatures that help me remember

ACKNOWLEDGMENTS

Special thanks to Aaron Moore MA, LMHC of Solace Counseling, Angie Winn,
and Reverend Cannon Patricia Orlando for their time reviewing these poems and
providing their generous endorsements. Thanks to my friends Seth Cain, Stephan
Monteserin, and Dana Roquemore for their time reading and providing thoughtful
feedback. Thanks to my writing community for the opportunities to read and share
these poems: The Florida State Poet's Association, Orlando Area Poets, Lauren White
and the Authentic Selves Poetry nights at Timucua Arts Center, and to the women in
my women's writing group at The Cathedral Church of Saint Luke in Orlando, Patricia,
Leslie, Iris, Elizabeth, Judy, Kathy. Thank you to Joy Rudolf and Reverend Katrina
Jenkins for their constant encouragement and support of my writing. Thank you to my
mother-in-law, Miki Jackson, and her sister, Becky Crawford for their cheerleading for
this latest book of writings. My mother is one of the great loves of my life. I have been
so grateful for their motherly presence in this season. Thank you to my boys Elliot and
Isaiah and their incredibly supportive father, Kyle, who has been present for me in
so many ways. I am in awe of the redemptive love we are experiencing after all these
years together. Special thanks to the Florida State Poets Association for publishing
the poems "All That is Green" (2022) and "Hands of Mercy" (2023) in their annual
anthology, Cadence, and to Joybird Books in Orlando for featuring me as a new author
in their store and selling pre-orders for this book. Thank you everyone at Finishing
Line Press for publishing this second book in the series of three. William Nicholson
wrote, "We read to know we are not alone." I write in hopes I am in good company.

Publisher: Leah Huete de Maines
Editor: Christen Kincaid
Cover Art: Angela Griner
Author Photo: Angela Griner
Cover Design: Elizabeth Maines McCleavy

Order online: www.finishinglinepress.com
            also available on amazon.com

Author inquiries and mail orders:
Finishing Line Press
PO Box 1626
Georgetown, Kentucky 40324
USA

Contents

Shame Is Not a Resting Place

Shame is not a resting place.
Shame is our meeting place.
Where we can see just how
luminous this Grace is.
How she enters the dark
with palms of peace at her feet
blessing her way with every step
closer to us. We are exposed, but
not mortified, stricken, but not lost.

With hands of mercy, she draws us in
closer, closer still and asks that we walk
with her back through the way she came.
She asks that we gather up the crushed
palms as we go, then sets them on fire
to light our way out When the fire burns out,
we are in darkness again for a time,
surrounded by the ashes of all that has been lost.

She meets us here
as many times as we need
and marks our hands, our feet, our foreheads
with these ashes. These are the combined
ashes of peace, sorrow, loss, and love.
These are the ashes that will bring us home.
Shame is not our resting place.
Shame is our meeting place
for Grace to bring us home again.

All That Is Green

All that is green
goes to the light
pushes up and out or over
whichever way will catch
So I too must go to the light
bring my frayed edges 'round
stretch them up and out
even if it means tearing
apart

I'll tremble and flow
expand and deflate
pumping it all
back down to
the ones I had to
leave behind

Good Night, Love

Like moonlight
all the vast array of colors
subdued into one fantastic
shade of night
Yesterday will reveal
a new light upon everything
For now, rejoice in the soft light
of the night-rest
your traveler's head and stay gentle
Gentle like the night sky
harboring her stars
without laboring herself
Good night, Love

I Am a Mother

I am a mother
Muscovy with her ducklings
I am a rescuer with her pups
nestled in on the couch
full of blankets and cushions
that will need another washing soon
I am a soft pink blanket soothing
her grieving girl
I am the perfume that whispers
the still presence of her mother
I am a seasoned observer
giving grace to the heron
while protecting her own
I am the god of stillness
laughter, easy grace
diligence, disbanding foreboding

A guiding hand scooping her
away from the worn edges
of past time on repeat
Bringing her to the low tide
of gentle waters, surrounded
bathed in and breathing in
the breath of the Beloved

Repentance

I am drawn into repentance
from ideas held from my long time past
from those held with my newfound identities
    to help me feel sane
    to help me feel safe
    to help me belong

For in these ideas I am beholden
to one kind of good
at the expense of many others
I become blindsided
so secured by this pinhole view
that I hardly see anything else
    one opposing idea creates its opposite
    one proclaimed identity denies another

We lower ourselves to ascend
I'm not talking about humility here
We lower ourselves to ascend in that
we set aside our humanity in an attempt
to be without flaw and this is not possible
not on this side of heaven and earth

I repent of ideas committed to separation
as futile attempts
    to be whole
    to be good
    to be righteous

Jesus brought the holy grail to show us
what it means to be human, the carpenter's cup
of crude and smoothed out carvings
shaped by hands that have learned
how to carry water and chop wood sparingly
with creature and family and land

in mind you cannot lose thought of one
for the sake of the other
each must be tended and considered

How do you shape the cup you've been given?
What grooves and handles will you carve for yourself?
Seek to live in such a way that there are no t-shirts
you can buy that speak your whole truth
no party that covers all the freedoms for all the peoples
Get your hands in the dirt with
someone you have stopped speaking to
Clean the river with family members
you have disowned

Hike the trek northward to catch the view
with someone from the other side
Sow and reap forgiveness in the land
within that you have tended well

May this be the territory you expand
with God's blessings bestowed
that you do no harm to others
as you plant the stakes of your tent
and make yourself a home

Movement

Love is with you
Love is waiting for you
here, asking you
for presence
Your life is a gift for
as long as it's given
This is your life
Surrender to it
Enjoy it
Nestle in
the marsh
Flow freely with the water
and the flight
Feed and take care
of your young
Nestle into the chest
of your beloved
Let easy laughter
come to you,
the hard guttural
kind too
Make way to hold
space for the grief
and then let it flow
out of you
transforming
into love

We Feed the Birds

Perhaps there is a desperate hunger within us
which compels us toward a tangible way to satisfy
the hunger of another being

Consider first, the muse of your own hunger
your longings to love and be loved well
to belong and survive and do more than survive

Sit with your hunger
eat and drink of the beauty around you
and you will be full

Perhaps with your empty stomach satiated
you will not be so compelled to stuff the mouths
of these creatures with your unhealthy offerings

Satisfy your soul hunger first
then, if you still feel you must
make a good effort to gather seeds and greens
instead of empty bread to bloat these stomachs

Feed your own hunger
drink in their ability to belong
to this surface, their ability to
feed themselves, to love and be loved
by the life they're given
Be fed well by your own life.

I Love My City Peace

I love the gritty turtles that overrun this tiny pond of a lake
in front of engines upon engines sounding out their particular
brand of pollution.

I love the red-tailed hawk trying to consume his next meal
with the anxious mockingbirds carrying on blisteringly overhead.

I love the mama duck who starts with 20 and ends with 2
and even the stoic blue heron, mercilessly contributing to each take
and the slimy, snouty soft shell taking from underneath.

This grimy lake of lawn fertilizer run off, a thousand different types
of oak leaves spilling into the sediment, along with the drainage from
that stiffening, soaked raccoon carcass blocking the storm drain, I love.

The neighbors with all of their dogs, and the waste some of them
leave behind in the recently soaked grass after the thousand rains
from the last two weeks that refused to let up.

I love the smell of jasmine and the bright pink bougainvillea
that will overtake everything eventually.

I love the graffitied bars and sticky floors and the way the sun and wind
will still dance and spread out across this water at sunset.

She, the Sun, loves—our grit, our grime, our color, our tenderness
our doubtfulness, our hope, our breathlessness, our breathe.
She knows our last leaf is coming and she keeps on shining.
What is love but seeing and relentless presence?

Dear lime green anole,

With the gash along your narrow head just starting to heal over. I saw you attacked yesterday, yet here you are on this old poolside deck with the screen hanging on one last side. Thank you for your beauty and resilience.

Sincerely,

Your sister in recovery

My Mother's Makeup Bag

I threw away my mother's make up bag today. I picked through which cheek brush was new enough to keep and used just enough to imagine these soft hairs on her cheeks now on mine, that I may somehow remain a little closer to her and to my longing.

I go through all the necessary intricate tools of beauty making for her tribe that kept her eyebrows in shape and her nails smooth. I find a few useful scissors to keep and extra pairs of tweezers and nail clippers to replace the ones my boys keep stealing from my own beauty keeping stash.

I see her hand-held mirror and that comb with the metal pick on one end to keep her hair as light and full as possible. I pull out all her serums and creams and wonder which ones I ought to start using as I'm now getting to that age- where fine lines and wrinkles matter in all the ways I said they never would.

There's a light coating of hair spray and Estée Lauder powder over everything and her long strands of hair tied in with each scrunchy and hair tie. I just want it all to blend together and conjure her up in real time presence.

My sweet, Pentecostal mother—gentle spirit, bafflingly organized, healer with well-manicured hands, and the face that held for me, my first image of God.

Hands of Mercy

I come into this room into your lost hands
the lines, wrinkles, curved bone on my shoulder
rubbing my back with your pearl-covered nails.
You hum a sweet tune with a southern sway
under your breath.
These are the hands and notes that taught me grace.

I strum the chords on your old Gibson
oils from your calloused fingertips to mine
each deep groove in the soft wood
holding its own song
This is my sacred recounting of you.

The record plays and you belt out
spools of mercy
for yourself, for your childhood
for your mama in that yellow house your papa built
for my father and his brother and your little girl
then, back round again to your own deepest need.

There you bore us hope in the new life
that was waiting for you once you broke
yourself free and gathered up the scattered pieces.
You brought them to us whole and
from your hands we ate
our need for love impeccable
acceptance soothed.

Your children's children and theirs
soothed by sacred love
brought by well-worn hands
freedom
no longer bound
to our ancestor's carriage
harboring the hurts of the dead
bringing us further into
the land of the living.

Handling

They took me and they held me down
over and over again until
they couldn't stand to see
another thing wrong with me.
Like pulling nits from my hair
my nose, my eyes
every last damn particle
that would make them
feel embarrassed
for themselves for what they were
and were not, for what they needed to be
and couldn't quite get a handle on
so, they handled me.

Twisted me up and wrung me out
saturated me with their own
bodily fluids and painful memories
not knowing they were committing
sins against humanity, not knowing
I was just a child, not knowing
what it was to be held or how to hold
only how to handle.

But once I saw this wasn't the way
it had to be for me and for my children
I began taking each wretched wrist
giving it back to its owner.
I began speaking love to each place
white and faded from lost circulation
blood and life to flow again
my own fluids filling me up
Each hand back to its origin.
Each piece back in its place.

Each star dust memory
brought back to the place
of remembering that I was
always a real girl
meant for embracing
no longer allowing herself
to be handled.

Avonlea's Antiques

I went to Avonlea's antique mall today
to have some cake and pick up knickknacks
and old photos, worn frames
and other odd old things
from the places
they've been set
laid out to sell.
My heart is here
on one of these shelves
waiting for me to find her
to pick her up
to hold her gently
in my hands and place her back
where she belongs
inside of me.

When I've finished
gathering up my collections
I sit down to have some cake.
I choose the piece my mother
would have chosen
with the ladyfingers
the raspberry cream
and white chocolate.
I ask for some coffee
I know will be a bit stale but
well suited for this moment.
I sit there, with my heart intact
weeping for all I've lost
and for the beauty
that has been collected
in this random place
of random things
over well-planned visits.

Some pieces of my mother
are lying round.
If you listen
you can hear
us laughing
and playing pretend.
You can hear me making
fun of a creepy doll or two
and observe my mother
happy to be with her girl.

If you are still and quiet
you may glimpse a passing chatter
of making future plans
and speaking of the past
amalgamations of memory and love,
tenderness, forgiveness too.

If you sit still
you can taste the sweet
the stale, and the bitter
and you will weep for joy
to feel your heart beating
so alive within yourself
present to what was
and still is
to the aching
of the loss
still and present
still and here
found and lost
in this place
of lost and found.

For Mothers and Daughters

A silk threaded ribbon woven
into the heart of this mother
born into the heart of this daughter
smooth, tender, slick
strong enough for cleaving
light enough to adjust
to each leaving that begins
when her toddler legs hit the floor
for the first time

Hidden love now stretched
outside the chest for all to see
some mothers will choose
to cling more tightly with every pull
some mothers will let go too soon
some will gently allow
this ribbon to pass through her hands
at her daughter's need
gathering up the slack
when holding is needed
letting out the spool
when more space is required.

Let this ribbon remain
within both mother and daughter
with grace and fluidity
let this ribbon remain
whatever the moment calls for
may there be gentle grace
blessing the other
in her glorious human form
to be free to be more of herself
the mother in a new season
the daughter in hers
blessing the bond between them
blessing the space between them
forgiving what needs forgiven
loving for the time that is now

God Is a Mother

It doesn't require much
just a glance
slight scent
faint sound
that puts a light
upon you
to tell you
you're mine

It is nothing
to point you
out in a crowd
to pull you out
from the piling chaos
to clasp you in safety
only a hint

Our Sons

Like trees in the ocean
rooted deep
in infinite history
and infinite becoming
our boys
one of my two
two of your three
here in this photo

Would we be here
together if we weren't
so completely separated
from you and are we
all that separate?

You and I have the same brow
the same deep-set eyes
just underneath
they reign in our sons
all five of them

You and I have the same tenderness
with our deeply set and outspread hearts
they reign in our sons
kings of hearts

We've wondered if we belong
here on this ocean floor
with our sons
barely breaking
the surface

We've wondered if we will survive
enough for them to emerge
and look, brother
they're here now

they've broken the surface
they are of the earth
and the ocean
they are of us

There are All Kinds of Love

There are all kinds of love in the world
                              in this world
                                     in my world
This pillow
      this pink pillow
            and yours
                  the teal one
                        my Sandy and her red hair
The love that comes
            out from regret
The hope that all isn't lost
            that there is still time
                  somewhere to find it

The love that comes blooming
            from random places
                  like cow dung
                        and the butterflies that fly around it
                              finding something holy about the whole
                              wild and perfunctory stench
                              the loveliness of it
the nourishment

In all the wildness
            dirt and yeast
                  butter and softness
                              decay

All the living things that come from and for this last gift offered
by death to push forth the next generation of something

Many kinds of love
      out from regret
            out from hope
                  out from the clinging and the stench that comes from
                  the sweat of the
                  clinging

out from the grace of good fortune too
        that still
           and still
              again comes

The many kinds of love
    the will to live
    the want to survive
    the way to find a way where there has been
none for so long
    the want you share to be out from it all
        the shame
          the spiraling
            the relief-temporary
              the pain that comes after
                constant and dependable

That's love too
  it's in there
    the hope of relief
    the hope that there's a salve
    the longing that meets the longing
      and offers the hint
      and hope of something else
          another way

That pain of regret is love
  love speaking to you again that there's something else
    That pain that brings you to this place on your knees
towards this quick fix
    again
      and again
      and again

There is love in that too
    calling you to yourself
    love, it's right there in the stench of it
    bearing down on you
    like a fluttering of holy kisses
    all over your smitten face

You are the love
    that bleeds to be found
you are the loved
    that cries to be heard
                    and seen
                            and remembered
You are the loving
    that will find her way to life

Life Is Never Wasted

Life is never wasted
unless you're working with a scale
you try fitting a newborn
in the arms of his mother
on one side and weighing it out
with that baby's lived fears
when he is grown

Life is never wasted
unless you're keeping score
You try and grade the progress
of a child learning to ride her bike
getting her untied shoestrings
tangled up in the pedals
on a curve with a privileged man
making his well buttered bread

Life is never wasted
unless you're comparing marks
who wants to lay down their body
for the surgeon's marks
all the things she would cut out
to make you well, whole, not wasted?
What is left then?

Not wasted parts, only wasted time
weighing out and marking
what is good and what isn't
situating oneself in the seat of judgement

Blessed is she who denies
the seat of the scornful
moves out of the way of sinners
walks in the river of unknowing
and extends the mercy given to her

to shut down the proclamations of men
naming what is empty and wasted
out from their tombs of rancor.

Nothing is wasted
no scales, marks, scores
can steal away
your preciousness
nothing gets wasted
alchemy
is always,
perpetually,
just around the bend.

The Heavy-Hooved Monster

Grief is a monster
heavy-hooved
bearing down
behind me I feel his
silent breathing
calculating
his next move
and
I feel
so very
small
like that time when I was 8
I woke up out of a dream, no, a night
terror, out of my bed and I couldn't find
the door. I was crying for my mother
screaming through the blinds
grasping for sight
there he was
at the foot of my bed and then again
right beside me
between me
and the door
to my parents who
were
just
across
the
hall

Grief is a monster
heavy-hooved
bearing down
and I am grasping for sight
screaming through the blinds
begging for the door

Rejection

When rejection is king
it feels like nothing else is good
that one human not seeing you well means
you do not deserve to be seen at all
When rejection is king
you lose your purpose
stomach for life
old grudges begged
to shake off
keep condemning
no path to love and be loved
well in return
When rejection is king
your only regret
is being who only you can be
to need is pity
to err means loss
When rejection is king
Death stands at your door
and offers relief
when rejection is king

The Harsher Sounds

The harsher sounds
of nature stand aside
to taunt me
the winter fog hides the sun
it is hard to breathe
hard to mother
myself and my children
with my mother gone from this world

Nature knows I love her and today she gives me this
what have I to do but be here now
with all my failures?
As I beg for favor
I beg for favor
I beg for favor
or mercy at least
give me mercy at the very least
and the sun shining all around me

This Is the Street Where I Once Lived

This is the street corner
where my parents lived
my brother across one street
my grandparents across another
me two hours away
(enough distance to claim my independence)

Later, the same street I would live on
for a little while with my first born
under the weight of disorienting depression
where I watched my brother get sober
and then un-sober again
where I walked the streets
with my baby on a front pack
begging to find a new
hope-filled normal

Where my brother found stray kittens
under his porch, and we took two of them
home with my then 5-year-old
who held them ever so gently

This is the street where fireworks
were let off as firsts for three different grandboys
where Nana and Papa raised a playhouse yard
with a pool, trampoline, and playground.

These are the sidewalks we traded
dishes and food between houses
on holidays and regular days
One common street corner
like so many random low-class
high-comfort neighborhoods
millions seemingly just alike
We were all here once
living, breathing, celebrating
struggling, surviving, thriving

It's all lost now-gone to the age of itself
and a new one is calling to me, one of the ones left
and to my grandmother, help me love well, my God
To count my losses with my blessings
let the sun set on these leafless branches
I will carry the memories with me to sleep
and wake up to a new kind of
hope-filled normal tomorrow.

If I Could be a Word

What word would I be?
Weighted beside you
Waiting beside you
Spoon on spoon
Feeding you warmth
and light
What could be both or all the things
to say, "You bring me life.
You bring me joy."

Once you brought me death.
Even then, you always brought
me coffee. What word says there
isn't enough time yet I choose
to spend it with you
all
day
long
everyday?

Silver hairs blowing in
from everywhere, laying
on my cheek resting on your chest.
What word speaks this forever and
always within this unknown?
What word says I pray the lord to
take my soul with thee, for never
a night to be spent without
me by your side
Weighted
Spoon on spoon
Feeding us warmth
and light

What is the word that tells more
of love than we ever knew?
That I lay myself down for this love
that brought, then conquered our death once
that must conquer it again another day?

What word can speak for me?
I cannot count the ways
I cannot speak your face
I cannot mouth your embrace
I sit a single being
pronouncement
of something great
some deep mystery
only we can know
yet we cannot utter

Like Yahweh
God's breath
our love
brought out from the chaos
lifted out from the depths
broken love made whole
God-breathed
yes, that's it
Yahweh
Yahweh
Yahweh

She is a Beast

Breathing
Sighing
Shaking
Swaying
Moving to the movement
Settling with the sediment
Rising with the rising
Falling in response

Green flutters
Brownish hues
The kind of breathing that comes with rest
The kind of sighing that comes with acceptance
The kind of shaking that comes with the shutter of what was
what might have been, to prepare for what is in front of her

Swaying like dancing that starts in the hips as all good dancing does
Moving in the flow of fingers in the water
on the piano rippling, rippling
Settling with the ashes
Rising with the heaving and the glory
Falling with each call of the wind
Fine-tuned to the conditions
This albatross at sea

Rain

White noise and silver lines
softening the heat
saturated atmosphere
cooling the breeze
calming the sun
subsiding to bring her back
dampening and cleansing
all that's been left behind

Angela Griner is a writer, artist, and educator living in Orlando, Florida with her husband, two boys 17 &11, three dogs, and one cat, teaching, writing, painting, and spending time outdoors. After several years teaching young children in elementary schools and earning her masters and doctorate in education, she began teaching educators through professional development and developing and implementing course work at UCF and Rollins College. She currently teaches courses centered on responsive and inclusive literacy practices in teacher education programs, along with studying the role of mental health, wellness, spirituality, and trauma-informed practices in teaching and learning, with creative expression as an integrative approach towards inclusive, healing centered pedagogies.

After experiencing several profound losses, she has found healing and joy through contemplative practices and creative expressions through music, writing, and art, that help her surrender and consent to life's unexpected gifts-both the light and the dark. Some of these darker gifts have included the loss of her brother to overdose, both parents, just two days a part to Covid, and other personal and family struggles with depression, suicide, trauma, addiction, betrayal, and loss. So far, she has found that nothing gets wasted and it is possible for recovery, redemption, and resurrection to hold the last words.

www.ingramcontent.com/pod-product-compliance
Lightning Source LLC
Chambersburg PA
CBHW020223090426
42734CB00008B/1188